Bells
—with—
Wings

Bells
with
Wings

Eileen Blakeman

ARCHWAY
PUBLISHING

Archway Publishing books may be ordered through booksellers or by contacting:

Archway Publishing
1663 Liberty Drive
Bloomington, IN 47403
www.archwaypublishing.com
1-(888)-242-5904

Because of the dynamic nature of the Internet, any web addresses or links contained in this book may have changed since publication and may no longer be valid. The views expressed in this work are solely those of the author and do not necessarily reflect the views of the publisher, and the publisher hereby disclaims any responsibility for them.

Any people depicted in stock imagery provided by Thinkstock are models, and such images are being used for illustrative purposes only. Certain stock imagery © Thinkstock.

ISBN: 978-1-4808-0628-3 (sc)
ISBN: 978-1-4808-0629-0 (e)

Library of Congress Control Number: 2014903746

Printed in the United States of America

Archway Publishing rev. date: 03/03/2014

To nature's gifts

Introduction

Okay, folks: so here I am, walking my dog, Molly, one early morning on Cape Cod.

It's springtime. The flowers are blooming; the trees are full of buds; the sound of birds are overhead. Mating has begun.

An idea lights up. Wow, I'm not that much different from that wild pink rose hidden from view, deciding if it wants to join this world or hide behind a wall of weeds. Or am I so different from the squeaking birds protecting and nurturing their offspring?

So what do we do that they don't do? Or what do they do that we don't do?

An interesting insight. I had to rush home to put a poem on paper lest I lose this delightful thought. So there you have it: my poems, bringing us closer to nature.

Eileen Kerr Blakeman

Poems

Enjoy 1

Lessons 2

Follow Me. 3

In Honor of Parents 4

Beauty on the Outside 5

Just for You .6

Cut Short 7

Relax 8

Awaken 9

Bath Time. 10

Lily Pods 11

Nature Protects 12

Mama 13

Vines 14

Truth 15

Questions 16

The Makings 17

By and By 18

A Trip 19

One Moment 20

Free Up 21

Just Saying 22

In Time 23

A Gathering. 24

Awakenings. 25

Always There. 26

Love All 27

Guess Who?. 28

Think Positive 29

Nature's Wishbone 30

Show Me 31

Forever 32

Cape Cod 33

Shawme Pond 34

East Sandwich 35

Then and Now 36

Giving Thanks 37

Wake Up 38

From a Distance 39

No 40

Greener Fields 41

Self-Love 42

Frog 43

Beware 44

Brighter Days. 45

Barn Swallows 46

No Freebies 47

October 48

Look about 49

Deception. 50

Rejuvenate 51

No Woodpecker 52

Our Time 53

Moss 54

Wishful Thinking 55

Autumn 56

Us 57

Maisy 58

The Coast 59

Loughview 60

Ghostly Love 61

Two Beauties 62

Pennington's Furniture 63

For Maude 64

A Message 65

Diversion 66

Sprinkle Love 67

Life 68

Sharing 69

Oh Yes, Oh No 70

Healing Prayer 71

This Desert 72

First Things First 73

A Tree Talks 74

Bobcats 75

Your Guess 76

Desert Fun 77

Sharing Life 78

New Law 79

Grateful 80

Ashes of Life 81

Maybe 82

Quiet Love 83

Being on Top 84

A Teabag 85

Nature's Way 86

Dust to Dust 87

Now 88

Watch Out 89

Rock Fun 90

Stay Alert 91

Keep Writing 92

Your Day 93

Jumping Spiders 94

Hello Memories 95

A Child's Poem 96

My Way 97

My Recipe 98

Enjoy

Step into my book of nature rhymes.
There are sad, colorful, and funny times
Where an almost-tear or a smile so faint
May make you late for a dinner date.

Lessons

Voices of nature speak out to me;
They wish to show me what they see.
So a flower blooms; vines with grapes.
A furry face or one with grace.
Come forth; speak up as best you can.
For life is now, so please do care.
I want to write and tell your part
Of things we do—but not like you.

Follow Me

How peaceful they are—
No stress well deserved.
They stand at attention,
No shrugging observed.
Nature teaches us a way
To live only by the day.
Heavy rain may descend—
Or the traffic of feet.
A time to defend
Brings a challenge to meet.
Come the sun and the warmth—
Carry on and stand tall.
Allow nature to show you:
Get up; go on from a fall.

In Honor of Parents

One, two, three, behind Mom and Dad.
We could have been a scrambled egg,
And so we wish to peep; we're glad.
We were told we could have been taken,
But Mom and Dad fought off the lad.
Our thanks for all you have forsaken,
The hours of love and warmth we had.
One, two, three, behind Mom and Dad.

Eileen Blakeman

Beauty on the Outside

Picture-perfect white swan,
I caught you in action
Chasing a mallard duck,
Who had a very sad reaction.
Out of the pond he had gone.
This world is for sharing.
So please back off a mile,
And let the duck come back
Quacking a big happy smile.

Just for You

How delicate they are,
Yet so strong to survive—
Beautiful pots of flowers in bloom.
Bring on the rain, torrential or not;
They fight for their right
To hold beauty for us.
Come the sun and warm rays,
Bringing forth a twinkle of a glow.
Our flowers are saying,
"Continue with life; we're here for you."

Cut Short

Dear clematis,
You were a dream
That never bloomed.
You died too soon,
With withering buds
Never to be
For me to see.

My lovely indigo,
I treasured you so.
Come back to me.
Twine up the fence.
Your life was cut short,
But your beauty I will see
In a dream of thee.

Relax

The rising perfume catches my nose.
The violet blossom captures my eye.
The enticing lilacs have a message to say:
Breathe in beauty; breathe out with a sigh.

Awaken

A speck of color caught my eye—
A beautiful wild rose spotted up high.
Covered in tall weeds, a view from behind
Brought a pensive thought to my mind.
Let out your beauty deep inside.
Show you to the world; do not hide.

Bath Time

Warm summer rain
And dirty black fur,
A shower is taken by her.
Running through a puddle,
Then back for a cuddle,
Fur dripping wet, right to her tail.
Molly's bark: what a happy wail.

Lily Pods

How peaceful they float,
As gentle as a breath of air.
Shimmering pink and white beauty
Radiate forth the power of peace,
While grouping together shows how
Sharing love, happiness, and sorrow
Binds the heart to feelings of the world.

Nature Protects

Bulrushes so strong,
Standing tall around the pond,
Protecting the frogs
Sitting on logs.

They jump and they rivet,
And by golly, they give it—
A scene or two
Of a mind-capturing view.

Mama

Little bird, little bird,
Your mama's nearby.
So anxious to be fed—
She is here up high.

Little bird, little bird,
Your mama's nearby.
Your wings do flutter;
You are one hungry guy.

Little bird, little bird,
Your mama's nearby.
With your beak so wide,
You swallowed with a sigh.

Vines

Climbing, climbing, climbing vines
Send exciting shivers up my spine.
The wonderful blooms, flower or food,
Put me in a romantic mood.
Whether it be grape, rose, bougainvillea,
Or trumpet vine, you pesky twine.
The power of love extends from east to west.
Enjoy their beauty along with a taste of wine.

Truth

I look at life.
I look at love.
Love is life;
Life is love.
A mate they are,
But not for life—
For love can part,
A break from life.

Questions

Floating gently—but where to go?
An urge to leave, but thoughts are so.
My mind goes round and thinks of you;
I shall miss your love, and tenderness too.
Contentless times will be questioned;
Restlessness will be shown.
I need a push to get me going,
So for now, my feelings are unknown.

The Makings

Run in the breeze;
Run through the trees.
Run, run, run—
Views for a poem she sees.

Views from afar,
Views aglow by a star,
Unimaginable views—
How quaint they are.

By and By

A fallen leaf
Floats on and on
Until the time
When it is gone
With passing thoughts.

Come back and join
This life we live.
The joys and sorrow
May come tomorrow,
But love is always
Here to give.

A Trip

You go in the dark;
You fly through the night.
You sigh with a smile
At the most awesome sight.

You awake with a yawn;
You remember your dream.
You're so glad you didn't wake
With a blood-curdling scream.

One Moment

It is such a day.
What can I say?
Carry on your way,
Or enjoy and stay.

Free Up

Come here; come near.
Let loneliness escape.
Allow joy to sweep in
Like a quick-moving tide
Washing out to sea—
The heartache of life.

Just Saying

If I were a monkey high up in a tree,
You would think I was on a lookout spree.
If I were a praying mantis on the ground,
You would think I was just grass all around.
If I were a spider in a swimming pool,
You would think I was a twig—you fool.
If I was me right where I belonged,
You would think my thoughts were never wrong.

In Time

Something good is going to happen;
I can feel it in my bones.
The thought of disappointments
Wants me to pick up sticks and stones.
Although I know that love shall abide,
I wish with all my might
The world will see my wondrous sight
And come to think along my side.

A Gathering

Wild spears of purple,
You display a pretty sight—
A view from afar.
I would give you a star.

The rustle of your laughter,
The sway of your dance
Bring me to be carefree
And walk with a prance.

Awakenings

I look up high and see the trees
Gently swaying in a summer breeze.
I pass a bush with the scent of rose—
The wonder of how fast it grows.
I look at life; I look at me:
The growth of wisdom I do see.

Always There

I wonder how my life will fare.
I wonder if he shall care.
The days are long;
The nights are dark.
I see his face above my stare.

Love All

Oh, morning glory,
Climbing the garden arbor,
Will you not be sorry?
For a grape vine has
Entwined opposite you.
A joining of fruit and flower—
A beauty meant to shower.

Guess Who?

Yellow bird, yellow bird,
Peeking out between
My black-eyed Susans,
Perching so sweet
Without even a tweet.

Yellow bird, yellow bird,
I spotted you there
With your piercing stare,
So pretty a picture;
Are you a him or a her?

Think Positive

A dream or two to dare
Of something gone—beware,
For thoughts will get
An anguished look
On a lovely face so set.

Nature's Wishbone

I pass a tree with a trunk so large
Extending its branches; a mighty two,
Wishing to all a life full of love,
Along with that good stuff only for you.
Now comes the happiness from within,
Bringing a smile with a great big grin.

Show Me

Fly away, little bird;
Fly high in the sky.
Bumblebee, I see you
Flying low to the ground.
The silence of the two
Brings me to ponder;
Their life is so peaceful,
Focusing on their world.
So I listen and take note—
A thought I just wrote.

Forever

There never is an end,
But only a beginning,
Be it days or years
Or life and death;
An end has a beginning,
And a beginning has an end.

Cape Cod

Every time I take a wondering turn,
I see a wavy green-leaf fern.
I think of basking on a pacific island.
Although I have for thirty years
Walked the shores of sea and sand,
I guess I may as well enjoy
And call right here my tropical land.

Shawme Pond

A glass of mystery, a magical pond beneath,
Holds the secrets of a small town.
The years of stories, drowned in sorrow,
Rise to the surface of past images.
The shadows from the water
Reflect through the crystal like glass
The key to life of years that pass.

Eileen Blakeman

East Sandwich

How quiet it is
With woods all around.
Come walk the neighborhood,
And perhaps you will say,
"This is a place where I shall stay."

Then and Now

Acres and acres of farmland,
Where cattle once did roam—
A thought of nature's love
Crossed my mind one August morn.
The end of summer, the end of a time
When cows would graze on lush grass
And bask along a country road fence.
Now a beautiful development
With two-story homes
Pass on the feelings of peace, once more.

Giving Thanks

A fallen branch has yet to rot,
A fallen soldier who once had fought,
Their lives did cease—but wait!
A dead log will always warm our hearts;
A soldier gone will be remembered,
Keeping our world safe till our last breath.

Wake Up

The sound of an alarm,
A rooster dressed with charm,
A feel of country—what a dream.
Let's shout and scream,
"Good morning, good morning,"
With a coffee and one cream.

From a Distance

I see a bird outside my window
Pecking rat-a-tat-tat.
I wonder if it wants my attention
Or just to tantalize my old cat.

I point my finger at the window;
Its head cocks from side to side.
My cat leaps from the sofa
And tends to want to go and hide.

With a wave of its wings
The bird flies off.
I guess it dropped by only to say,
"Hello, old cat, I must not stay."

No

You peeked your face
Out beneath the rocks
And scared my customers
Out of their socks.

You smooth, slithery,
Black-and-white snake,
Stay away from my shop
For goodness' sake!

Greener Fields

There is a secret path I take
To sit and ponder in the woods.
I think of times that could have been
Without a thought or two so mean.
I stand about the trees and look
And see him gathering for the cold,
Awaiting winter storms, I am told.
Walking back home, I think of me,
Where cans of food are lined, one, two, three—
I come to think that wherever I will be
Life is the same as the squirrel in the tree.

Self-Love

One lonely red rose
Now a crimson pink,
Pampered with coffee grounds,
Sprinkled with care.

I cannot help but stop and stare.
Its vibrancy radiates out to all.
Treasure and love yourself;
Be the belle of the ball.

Frog

I see you there so still,
As quiet as can be.
You wait and wait until
There is no trace of me.

So sorry to intrude.
This garden is to view.
I shall not be so rude
To sneak a peek at you.

Beware

Sneeze! Sneeze!
Who's there, please?
Goldenrod, goldenrod!
Gently I will trod.

Brighter Days

Did someone lose a small white feather?
I hear tonight will bring cold weather.
Huddle up; stay cozy and warm.
This night shall pass; the sun will rise.
Did someone lose a small white feather?
I hear tonight will bring cold weather.

Barn Swallows

The wind and the rain,
The rain and the wind—
Flying through the sky.
Please get us there,
Oh mighty one up high.

Here we go from east to west.
The Mission is waiting,
Inviting us there to nest.
So come along; fly with us,
And enjoy a warm winter's rest.

No Freebies

Come pick free apples from my tree.
It's better than a store-bought fee.
Come one, come all; but do not stall,
For an apple-worm may peak its head:
"Go away, go away. This is my home;
Buy your apples somewhere instead."

October

Trod, trod, up the hill.
The air is quiet
And so still.
The sun is out
But yet so cool.
It's cold; it's cold;
I am no fool.
Back home, I say,
Where I will stay.

Look about

Dear sweet creatures,
Be always on guard,
For hawks that fly
Will take you by
Their beak so strong.
It may seem wrong,
But is life not so fair
For me not to care?

Deception

An innocent partaking
For all those that partook:
A bunch of purple berries
Taunting us like those we grow.
Life tells us to be cautious,
For who likes feeling nauseous?
A check on who we newly meet
Close by across the street.

Rejuvenate

I notice how sleepy our flowers have become;
Their petals have curled and dropped—some.
Another few with half a yawn
Are anxious to bed down,
As it is way past dawn.
Although we love to look and admire,
It is time for indoors and into our nest,
For our flowers need their beauty rest.

No Woodpecker

Tap, tap, tap, tap,
You're eating my barn.
I hear you inside,
Tapping on one side.

Tap, tap, tap, tap,
You're eating my barn.
Fly away and hide,
Or you will go for a ride.

Our Time

How beautiful they are in the fall,
Weeds of color bright and tall.
So quietly enjoyable, they come alive
And show a smile—we did survive!
Your nasty Roundup missed a spot.
I guess the weather was just too hot.

Moss

You look so pretty
In your green velvet skirt,
Sitting in the woods
Being such a big flirt.

You caught my eye
While walking by,
And with my camera here,
I had to stop and say hi!

Wishful Thinking

They look so warm and fuzzy.
I wish that this was true,
For life can throw a curveball
And knock you with a fall.

Autumn

Sprinkle your color; show your love.
Heads will turn and stand in awe
At the beauty of fall in all its glamor,
A showpiece of nature at its best.
Breathe in the context and relax with joy.

Us

We love the peace and quiet,
The sun shining on our back.
Enjoyments we have in common
Bring a sleep we do not lack.

We often walk alone,
Or sometimes in a pair.
With either two or four legs,
The love of nature we do share.

Maisy

One lone daisy
Bent over from the rain:
Bedraggled-looking flower,
I think I'll call you Maisy.

One lone daisy
Surviving summer's heat:
You're missing two petals—
I think I'll call you Maisy.

One lone daisy,
So strong and bold you are:
Smiling so sweetly,
I think I'll call you Maisy.

The Coast

It's Ireland at its best:
So green and wet
Along the Irish Sea,
You can see me here
Breathing in the damp air.

It's Ireland at its best:
The sheep and cows
Grazing in their pasture,
The roaring sea
With the air so sharp.

It's Ireland at its best:
Always presenting a test
For its hardy souls
Who live here in its beauty
And love it with a grin.

Loughview

Oh Loughview—I dream of you
Attached so strongly to the past.
Its Irish beauty escapes,
A feeling of belonging.
Although it was so long ago,
It's still my father's house.

Ghostly Love

I wake upon an Irish morn
A country where my dad was born.
I see them there, the house they had.
My dad, his family gone—so sad.

I walk along through the rain
To my father's parents' grave.
The cemetery full of souls
Wraps me in a rolling mist.

Do photos lie? I wonder why
A heart was placed
So silently upon my face.
I wake upon an Irish morn.

Two Beauties

Hello, sweet swans.
I have no bread,
So venture on;
Eventually you will get fed.

Eileen Blakeman

Pennington's Furniture

A family store
There is no more.
A shell of life
Left boarded closed.

A face of bricks
Looks out to me:
A glow of past,
So very little left to see.

It stands forever,
And seen by whomever
Who wants to remember
A little history of mine.

For Maude

So special in my heart—
Although we had not met,
I know I often thought of you
With love and kindness too.

I am a little late
To hug and tell you so,
But I think you're here among us
To whisper, "Yes, I know."

The silence of this moment,
The peace I feel—so true—
Brings gentle thoughts and memories
Of love just meant for you.

A Message

A gentle wind blew by.
I quickly turned
And saw you there,
The one who knew
That life of mine.
A breeze so quiet
Of times so fine,
I wonder how
The wind got hold
Of stories often told.

Diversion

The wind on my cheek,
A tingle, makes me think
Of days before,
My life a bore.

So walk five miles
In new shoes;
Then think about
That blistering sore.

Sprinkle Love

How warm is the sun
On an autumn day?
How warm is my heart?
I cannot say.
A passing thought
Floating above
Is filled with tender love.

Life

Winter will soon be here—
The end of another year.
I trod along in this life
And deal with an unknown strife.
I feel a pull within my heart
And wonder where I shall start.
To ask for help, I look above
And always get the same reply:
Give yourself your needed love.

Sharing

I come across a quiet bog.
So alive and free I do feel!
Cranberries scattered.
Hmm ... Shall I steal?
I think of winter—a fox or deer—
Perhaps I will leave them here.

Oh Yes, Oh No

The first snowfall of the year
Brings a joyful and sad tear.
The excitement of the holidays
Combined with anxious memories
Causes my thoughts to jump and say,
"How will I get through stressful days?"

Healing Prayer

She stole my soul deep within me.
My feelings are lost; no beauty I see.
The depths of my inner core
Spill over in sores so raw.
All thoughts of darkness to thaw ...
Please, the one who gave me life,
Come forth with brightness to begin.
Bring back my gentle, loving grin.

This Desert

The coyotes are howling.
The night is dark, a little cool.
The stars have not come out as yet.
This is the desert which I have met.

The wind has blown a gush of sand.
Skin so delicate is creased and aged
With dryness of a mouth so set.
This is the desert which I have met.

The moon so large and very round,
Its orange beauty for all to see.
The sky, a pink and blue—you bet
This is the desert which I have met.

First Things First

A sad little eye
Looked out with a stye.
It must be sore—oh my!

Come here, little one!
Some healing before fun—
Then up and off and run.

A Tree Talks

As I walked by
A yucca gave me two fingers.
Peace in the desert
Brings peace in my heart.

Stand tall and proud,
For whoever you are:
Accept no bullying
Here nor afar.

Bobcats

They come out at night
Staying out of your sight.
You see a large print,
Which gives you a hint.
They're hunting for dinner—
Perhaps a winner:
Yes. A rat and some scraps.
How happy they are!
No sign of the traps.

Your Guess

A whale of a rock
Of a prehistoric age,
Wonders of the desert
To fill a full page.
A view to enjoy,
But be careful to touch—
Oops! A rattler on such
A whale of a rock.

Desert Fun

The rabbits are out;
The rabbits are out.
Hop and play
Before the new day.
Outsmart the fox.
Fool the coyote.
Wiggle your tail
At the descending hawks.
The rabbits are out;
The rabbits are out.

Sharing Life

Two rocks they were
Of a jealous nature
Sitting side by side.
"Come climb on me!"
"No, come climb on me!"
They argued back and forth.

Till one day they saw their fate:
They had become so full of hate.
Eventually they heard *the* sound
And slowly tumbled to the ground.
To stay on top, you must not fight.
Don't drop down to the lowest height.

New Law

Trappers of bobcats,
Think humanely.
Get rid of your trap,
For soon you will
Be taking the rap.

Desert bobcats, cry out
For the right to say,
"Hey, we were given life
From the one we call He
To be admired for all to see!"

Grateful

The sun is out
On a dry desert day.
Our solar panels
Are at work—hooray—
Bringing nature's heat
To shower us with a
Well-deserved treat.

Ashes of Life

After I'm gone,
Let them go with the wind
To far away places
With unknown faces.

After I'm gone,
Let them ride with the waves
To a land of sun
Where life had begun.

After I'm gone,
Let them grow with the trees
To spread roots of love
To meet with the above.

Maybe

On my walk back
I spotted a snail—
A slippery, slimy
Shell with a tail.
A snail with a tail?
Perhaps my eyes
Are beginning to fail.
On my walk back
I spotted a snail.

Quiet Love

Good morning, my love.
The birds are awake, flying above.
The sun is slowly rising up.
I'm sitting enjoying my tea in my cup.

Good morning, my love.
While breathing in the morning dew
And perfume from flowers so few,
I'm sitting enjoying sweetness so true.

Good morning, my love.
The feeling of warmth on my back
Brings a closeness we do not lack.
I'm sitting enjoying our view with you.

Being on Top

Climbing the hill in the rain,
Oops—falling down this terrain.
Getting up and trying again,
Thinking, "Hmm, this is insane."
Climbing up, climbing down,
Climbing low, climbing high:
Don't mask your face of a clown.

A Teabag

It comes housed two in one,
The paper and the tea.
For me to write a poem of fun
On paper, drinking tea,
For now you see that's all it takes
To write a poem for me.

Nature's Way

Stars appearing in the night
Bring me to this wondrous sight.
Their twinkling glow leads the way
For those awaiting a new day.

They beckon you to look up high
Out in the night to the sky
And count the sheep
To gently put you back to sleep.

One lone star waits patiently
For a restless you and me
To close our eyes and with a yawn
Sleep tight all through till dawn.

Dust to Dust

While cleaning in the desert
You see a thin film of dust.
Here a duster handy is a must.
You dust and sweep all the day,
And finally you begin to say,
"This is the earth where we will go,
So let it sit and rest and stay."

Now

The shell of life
Is only but a page
Of things we did
And things we didn't.
The time is now,
Not of the past.
So write a page
Of beautiful thoughts,
The ones you saw
On your walk with Ma or Pa.

Watch Out

The house on the hill
Atop a rocky view,
So quiet and still,
Protecting all of you—
Or is it just
The king of the castle
And you're the dirty rascal?

Rock Fun

I went on a mission
To find a rock—
A rock with a chair
That had a stair.
I found the rock
That had a step,
A rock of a chair
With a step of a stair,
Sat only a step out there.

Stay Alert

It was almost dusk
When a pack of coyotes
Crossed my path.
I stopped to stare.
I did get a little scare
While on my walk,
Although it was the rabbits—
They were about to stalk.

Keep Writing

My goal was to write
One hundred poems.
All I wrote was ninety-three—
Except for ninety-four,
And if you turn the page,
There may be more.

Your Day

Around the corner
Is just another day.
Around the corner
There is so little to say.
Around the corner
There is a shiny ray.
Around the corner
Leads you on your way.

Jumping Spiders

I was reading a book late at night
When a spider crawled over my face.
It itched my nose and came into sight
On the edge of a newly turned page.
I jumped at the sight and closed the book,
Not knowing if it was captured in its cage.
The book, outside, took awhile to inspect.
Was it a scorpion? I didn't know what to expect.
It was only a desert spider, with a colorful look—
But well preserved inside the pages of my book!

Hello Memories

A glimpse of the past
Often brings a sadness
That will momentarily last,
While rethinking special times
Then written in my rhymes.

A Child's Poem

There is a little bird
That sits upon my head.
It waits and waits
For it to be fed.

There is a tiny mouse
That sits by my feet.
It sits and sits
Keeping warm in my house.

There is a red ladybug
That sits on my finger.
It clings and clings
Waiting for a big gentle hug.

My Way

Was it only yesterday?
When I was a child
I rescued a baby bird
And nestled it in hay.

Was it only yesterday?
I spotted a lame chicken;
I tended it with loving care
Until it came to hop a stair.

Was it only yesterday?
I found a homeless cat.
I brought it to my home
Deciding it must stay.

And yes, it is today.
I care about them all
And love them in a special way.
What more is there to say?

My Recipe

I go for a walk.
I bring home a poem.
I wrap it in my soul.
I carry it in my mind.
I write it for you.
I hope it is read.
I thank you.

www.ingramcontent.com/pod-product-compliance
Lightning Source LLC
Chambersburg PA
CBHW030346290526
45785CB00004B/1623